The Arabs – The Conflict

Jeffrey D. Johnson

Wipf & Stock
PUBLISHERS
Eugene, Oregon

Wipf and Stock Publishers
199 W 8th Ave, Suite 3
Eugene, OR 97401

The Arabs--The Conflict
By Johnson, Jeffrey D.

ISBN 13: 978-1-55635-076-4
ISBN 10: 1-55635-076-7
Publication date 11/30/2006

About Israel Today Ministries

Three-fold Purpose:

- Teach the Church about Israel
- Teach Israel about their Messiah
- Help feed those in need (Romans 15:27; Genesis 12:1-3)

To receive Dr. Johnson's "teaching letters," or, if you would like to send a gift to Israel Today Ministries, or if you would like Dr. Johnson to speak at your church event, school, or small group, contact:

Israel Today Ministries
P.O. Box 150288
Arlington, TX 76015
Phone/Fax 817.468.4441
E mail: Galileeman@juno.com

This is Yossef (Joseph) and Abigail. Your monthly donations help feed little ones like these.

"Inasmuch as ye have done it unto one of the least of these my brethren, ye have done it unto me" –Jesus, Matthew 25:40

About Dr. Jeffrey D. Johnson

- Three decades in ministry
- Founder/Director of Israel Today Ministries
- Director of tours to the Middle East
- Senior pastor in Ohio, Massachusetts and California
- Almost 7 years directorship with International Ministries to Israel (formerly, The American Association for Jewish Evangelism, where the famed Hyman Appelman was the first president)
- Conference speaker
- Bible expositor
- Guest lecturer
- Author

Born and raised in the Midwest, Dr. Johnson took his B.D. from Massillon Baptist College, his MA from Moody Bible Institute, and his Th.M. and Th.D. from Christian Bible College. His passion for Israel, the Jewish roots of Christianity and Bible prophecy, is well known. His teaching will stir your heart to follow the Lord and to love and *"pray for the peace of Jerusalem"* (Psalm 122:6).

As an "Itinerant Bible Teacher," Dr. Johnson will travel anywhere to proclaim God's redeeming Grace through our Lord and Savior Jesus the Messiah, *"to the Jew first, and also to the Greek"* (Romans 1:16).

His call is to *"Teach the Church about Israel; Teach Israel about their Messiah; and to feed those in need"* (Genesis 12:3; Romans 15:27).

Dr. Jeff and his wife, Louise, have purposed to serve the Lord trusting God to provide the funds and resources for their livelihood.

Israel Today Ministries, founded by Dr. Johnson, is a faith ministry, supported by "love offerings" from those desiring to bless Israel. Dr. Jeff and Louise have been commissioned and sent out by their home church.

Comments from Christian Leaders

I am pleased to recommend him to churches as an able expositor of the Word of God.

– *the late* **John Walvoord**, Chancellor,
Dallas Theological Seminary

A Bible Expositor with special insights on the origin, nature and destiny of God's chosen people, Israel.

– **John C. Whitcomb**, Bible Scholar, Author, Professor

A careful expositor of Scripture.

– **Homer Kent**, President Emeritus,
Grace College and Seminary

A practitioner of all that he preaches.

– **Paige Patterson**, former President of the
Southern Baptist Convention, President,
Southeastern Baptist Theological Seminary

He has a wonderful grasp of Jewish history and liturgy.

– **Edgar C. James**, Professor, Moody Bible Institute

He is a person who has been uniquely prepared by God to preach and teach about God's special people. Any one who hears him will come away with a great love for the people of Abraham.

–**Dick Dahlquist**, Chair, Pastoral Studies, Acting Dean,
Grace College of Graduate Studies

He has a gifted teaching ministry which encompasses Biblical prophecy and insights into modern-day Judaism.

–the late **Paul Tassell**, Bible Scholar, Author,
former National Representative of the G.A.R.B.C.

He has a great ministry.

– **LaVerne Butler**, former President of Mid-Continent Baptist College, Scholar, Conference Speaker, President, Pulpit Aflame

Your heart will be thrilled as he ministers the prophetic Scriptures.

– the late **Alden A. Gannett**, President Emeritus of Southeastern Bible College, Bible Scholar, Author, Conference Speaker, President, Gannett Ministries

He loves the people and nation of Israel. He has given himself to a thorough study of God's ancient people and of the prophetic.

– **Ivan H. French**, Pastor Emeritus, Pleasant View Bible Church, former Professor, Grace College and Seminary

Table of Contents

Chapter 1
The Conflict

Fearing the power of the Pharaoh, and the thought of losing his life, Abraham lied and stated that the extremely beautiful Sarah was not his wife (Genesis 12:10-16). Shortly thereafter, Sarah ended up in Pharaoh's home. He was courting her for marriage. Abraham now had a precarious situation on his hands.

Hagar

Subsequently, Pharaoh treated Abraham well and gave him what was really a bride price. The great Pharaoh thought Abraham was Sarah's brother. Basically, he was giving Abraham payment to marry his sister.

Once Pharaoh found out that Sarah was Abraham's wife he let her go and told them to leave his presence immediately. Abraham kept the bride price given to him by Pharaoh

Part of the bride price was a number of female servants. One of the servants was none other than Hagar (Genesis 12:16). Therefore, in verse 16, we have the first mention of the origin of the Arab peoples, through Hagar.

The Prophecy

God promised Abraham children through Sarah in chapter 12 of Genesis. However it had been over a decade since the promise was given. Sarah had given Abraham no children.

It was considered a curse from God to be barren. Sarah was confused and frustrated, and in accordance with the customs of their culture she offered her husband her maidservant (Genesis 16:1-6). The name of the Egyptian female servant was Hagar.

Hagar conceived resulting in great tension between Hagar and Sarah. Hagar felt her life was being threatened by Sarah and fled. An angel appeared to Hagar in the desert and reassured her and told her to go back to Sarah. He promised her that she would have a son and that she should name him Ishmael, which means, "The Lord Hears", and that her seed would be multiplied. God heard Hagar's cry in the wilderness and comforted her.

The Angel of the Lord gave Hagar 4 prophecies concerning her son Ishmael and his descendants (Genesis 16:12).

1. ***He will be a wild man***
   The descendants of Ishmael will be like a wild donkey, a nuisance wherever they would go.

2. ***His hand will be against every man***
   Aggressive, disorderly, a fighting propensity describes the progeny of Ishmael.

3. ***Every mans hand against him***
   History verifies this statement.

4. ***And he shall dwell in the presence of all his brethren***
   Meaning he will live in the face of or in defiance of or in hostility toward his brethren the Jew (descendants of Isaac).

Isaac

Some thirteen years later, after Ishmael was born, Sarah did conceive and bore Abraham a son, named Isaac. Isaac was God's promised son, the one who was to receive the blessing and inheritance. He was the son God referred too in chapter 12.

Eventually tension began to develop between the two brothers Ishmael and Isaac. As a result God then instructed Abraham to release Hagar and Ishmael, to have them leave his home. Nevertheless, the Lord guaranteed Abraham that He would bless Hagar and make a great nation through Ishmael. And indeed God did bless Ishmael's seed.

It is said, that if you take the land size half of Canada, half of Mexico and all of the United States, you will have the land mass area of the Arab nations. You take the land size of New Jersey you will have the land mass area of Israel.

Four sons – Two Nations

In Genesis 25 we find the story of Esau. The Arabs also consider themselves descendants of Esau. Rebekah, Isaac's wife, gave birth to twins, Jacob and Esau. Esau was born first, thus making him entitled to the inheritance of the covenant made to Abraham in Genesis 12. However, in chapter 25:34 Esau gave up his inheritance for a bowl of soup. Subsequently, Jacob the second born became the recipient of the inheritance.

Four sons have been mentioned: Ishmael, Isaac, Esau and Jacob. What does this all mean? How does it play out?

1. *Ishmael,* was Abraham's firstborn through the Egyptian maidservant Hagar. However, he was not the promised son. Ishmael's progeny are the Arabs. The Lord gave four prophecies concerning Hagar's son. (see The Prophecy above)

2. *Isaac,* was the promised son to Abraham through Sarah. He was the miracle baby, born to a woman who was past the age of childbearing years. Isaac's progeny are the Jews. The Messiah would come through his seed.

3. *Esau,* was Isaac's firstborn twin son through Rebekah. He would have received the inheritance, however, he gave it to his younger twin for a bowl of soup. He lost the inheritance. Arabs also claim to be descendants of Esau.

4. *Jacob,* was Isaac's second born twin son through Rebekah. He received the inheritance from Esau. Jews are also descendants of Jacob.

The Argument

Looking at this brief history of these four sons you find something very peculiar. Notice, the inheritance had gone to the second born son each time. Hmmm! God's ways are not our ways. His thoughts are not our thoughts (Isaiah 55:8).

The argument in the Middle East is who owns the land of Israel. The Arabs say they do. The Jews say it belongs to them. There are three main components to this argument:

The Family Argument

This tension between the Jews and Arabs goes back four thousand years. Abraham had two boys, Ishmael and Isaac. These two families have been fighting from the beginning. First we find that Sarah treated Hagar harshly in Genesis 16:6. Then Ishmael began mocking baby Isaac (2 or 3 years old) in Genesis 21:9. Notice the word translated *"mocking"* is a Hebrew word that means laughing or jesting. The word is a derivative of *"Yitzchak"* or Isaac, which means, "He will laugh". He was mocking the promised son. Perhaps, Ishmael (16 or 17 years old) was making fun of Isaac's name.

Then there are the twins of Isaac and Rebekah, Esau and Jacob. From the womb they were fighting and struggling with each other. Jealousy, deception, and quarreling describe their relationship (Genesis 25-36).

The descendants of Isaac and Jacob are the Jews. The descendants of Ishmael and Esau are the Arabs. So basically you have a family feud that has been lasting about four thousand years.

The Cultural Argument

Technically, the Arabs are correct, in that culturally a family's inheritance belongs to the firstborn son. Therefore, Ishmael and Esau should have received the blessing promised to Abraham and to Isaac. However, Isaac was the promised son, not Ishmael. And, Esau, gave away his birthright to his brother Jacob. Therefore, the blessing and inheritance had gone to Isaac and Jacob.

Yes, *culturally*, the inheritance should have gone to the firstborn. However, *biblically*, the inheritance was given to the second born. God's ways are not our ways, His thoughts are not our thoughts. God's ways are superior to any cultural distinctive or expectation.

The Religious Argument

Centuries after the resurrection of Jesus the Koran was written, Islam's holy book. Within its pages, Sura 2:124-129, you will read that Abraham bound Ishmael, instead of Isaac, upon the altar on Moriah. This would imply that Ishmael was the promised son of Abraham, thus the recipient of the inheritance. Also, this would imply that the Bible's account of Abraham binding the other son is incorrect. Of course the Bible is correct, and within the writings of Holy Writ, we read that it was Isaac who was bound upon Moriah, not Ishmael, in Genesis 22.

The Forefathers

So in the final analysis, Ishmael and Esau, the firstborn are the forefathers of the Arab peoples. Isaac and Jacob, the second born, are the forefathers of the Jews. So now we understand why there is tension in the Middle East and why there is fighting over the land of Israel.

Who owns the land? The descendants of Ishmael and Esau, the forefathers of the Arabs? Or, does the land belong to the descendants of Isaac and Jacob, the forefathers of the Jews?

Abraham fathered two nations. The Scripture tells us that the inheritance belongs to the descendants of Isaac and Jacob, namely, the Jews, regardless of the family, cultural or religious arguments.

The Solution

- *Politicians* will *not* solve the problems in the Middle East. It is not a political problem.
- *Soldiers* will *not* solve the problems in the Middle East. It is not a military problem.
- *Religious* radicals will *not* solve the problems in the Middle East. It is not a religious problem.

- *Messiah will* solve the problems and bring peace! Messiah Jesus will bring peace in two ways:

    1. **Personally** – Those who put their faith and trust in the Lord Jesus for the forgiveness of sins will receive eternal life with God. They will experience peace and will begin to love their neighbor. (John 3:16, 36; 13:35; Acts 16:31)

       I have seen both Jew and Arab worshipping the Lord together in peace, truly loving one another. Within the construct of the Body of Christ there is true peace and love.

    2. **Globally** – When we pray, *"Thy Kingdom come, Thy will be done on earth, as it is in Heaven"* we are praying for peace. (Matthew 6:10) When we pray for the peace of Jerusalem (Psalm 122:6), we are praying "Thy Kingdom come."

       So may we be faithful in praying for the peace of Jerusalem, thus, praying "Thy Kingdom come, thy will be done…" There will be no peace until the Prince of Peace comes.

This is the answer to the conflict. Jesus is the answer!

"Even so, come Lord Jesus" (Revelation 22:20)

"Time is Short; Life is Precious & Jesus is Coming Soon!

Chapter 2
The Clanging of the Swords
Matthew 24:4-8

In an hour in which military regimes are threatening the destruction of Israel, "clanging their swords" in hatred against the nations of the West and Zionists, how are we to interpret these thunderous clouds on the horizon? When nefarious dictators say they receive direct communication from God, rather, I should say, "a god", and this god tells them to destroy human life in the name of their cause, how should Christians respond? Are these the last days? Is the end near?

The disciples, in the shadow of the towering Roman Empire, facing oppression and threats on every side, asked Jesus, "When will these things be: And what will be the sign of Your coming, and of the end of the age" (Matthew 24:3)? Looking over the Kidron Valley, sitting on the Mount of Olives, gazing upon the beautiful marble, gold framed majestic Temple, that Herod renovated, Jesus communicated to his followers a profoundly succinct, sobering, yet comforting outline of future events. For our purposes today we will look at the first five verses of the Lord's answer.

Some theologians do not find the church in Matthew 24 & 25, due to the similarity between Matthew 24:4-7 & the six seals of Revelation chapter 6 which describes events in the Tribulation Period. Plus the disciples were perplexed as to Jesus predicting the destruction of the Temple, predicated by denouncing the religious leadership at that time (Matthew 23; 24:1,2). The disciples wondered how Jesus would rule in a Messianic Kingdom if the Temple was destroyed. Therefore, the questions asked were related to the Kingdom age and not the Church age.

On the other hand, some theologians believe that Matthew 24:4-14 refer to general signs of the end of the Church age, and beginning with verse 15 references regarding the beginning of the Tribulation. Whether the text describes specifically events relating to the Tribulation Period, or general signs regarding the end of the Church age, the principles are plainly understood. Therefore, let's simply explore what Jesus was saying in Matthew 24:4-8.

Three questions Matthew 24:3:

1. *When will these things be?* – The first question was answered in the synoptic passage found in Luke 21:20-24.

2. *What will be the sign of Your coming?* – The second was answered in Matthew 24:29-31.

3. *What will be the sign of the end of the age?* – This question will be our focus. What sign, or signs should we look for that clearly determines for us that the end-time clock has begun to tick? How do we know? The Lord answers the third question in verses 4-8.

4,5 For many will come in My name...and deceive

The Lord first tells us what not to mark as the beginning of the end of the age in verses 4-6. Jesus was the first to claim to be the Messiah. He proved the veracity of his claim via the resurrection. Bar Kokhba (ca. 132) was the next to claim Messiahship. Since then, there have been multitudes asserting to have special revelations from God. Many have stated they were the Messiah, others professed special, secret information, codes and mission deceiving and in some cases literally destroying the lives of multitudes. Today, the world is replete with cults, false teachers, and fanatics claiming to have direct communication with God. *But the end is not yet.*

6 Wars and rumors of wars

"Wars and rumors of wars" will happen. It is simply the propensity of humanity. Jesus refers to local, tribal, neighboring conflicts. World history verifies the fact that wars of this nature always happen. Do not be troubled, for *all these things must come to pass, but the end is not yet.*

7 Nation will rise against nation and kingdom against kingdom

This is a Jewish idiom that refers to "Global Conflict" or "Universal Fighting". In the Talmud (Jewish oral law and commentary that has been written) we read in Bereshit Rabbah 42:4, "When you see the kingdoms fighting against one another look and expect the foot of the Messiah." The disciples understood Jesus to be talking about conflict larger than tribal. Perhaps their minds reflected on the passages within Scripture referencing such larger conflicts as found in Isaiah 19:1-4 & 2 Chronicles 15:1-7. These passages talk about kingdom against kingdom, nation against nation, city against city, neighbor against neighbor and brother against brother. Complete breakdown of society at war with each other – global, or universal in context.

What follows such events are famines, pestilences and in this case earthquakes. These three will be manifested with obvious, growing intensity. The Twentieth Century birthed global conflict with WWI & WWII. The statistics have proven that the number of famines, pestilences, and yes, earthquakes had broken the records of previous history. Now, at the dawn of the 21st Century, the records continue to be broken in these areas.

Hating God

Currently, the nations of the world are choosing sides regarding the State of Israel. Thundering war clouds are on the horizon. Israel's prophetic rebirth in the 20th Century has heaved the world up against the fortress of God's "Logos". The citizens of planet earth do not appreciate that God's

Word is true, and that His chosen people are back in the land as He promised. The nation's hatred is against God. They just don't know it. They think it is against the Jew. They fight against God and His Word. (The world will loose). The land grant promised to Israel is much bigger than their current boundaries. It is simply a matter of time before they embrace completely their inheritance.

The Key

The Middle East is the key to understanding Bible Prophecy, specifically Israel, and more specifically Jerusalem. The holy city is the trigger that will unleash the wrath of the nations leading up to Armageddon. Global, universal conflict has begun. The prophetic clock is ticking. *All these are the beginning of sorrows.*

So now, what do we do?

Obviously, we are living in a very unique time unprecedented in history. The earmarks of the beginning of the 21st Century reflect a biblical paradigm of prophetic proportion. How then should we respond? How should we live?

1. *See that you are not troubled (Matthew 24:6; John 14:1-3)* – knowing these things were written ahead of time we should not be deceived. Comfort rests in the knowledge that God is in control. The world is not spinning out of control, though it seems like it is in a state of chaos. God's plan for the ages is beginning to unfold. The Kingdom is near!

2. *Now when these things begin to happen, look up (Luke 21:28)* – in the parallel text of Luke's gospel Jesus reminds the disciples that when these horrible events in world history take place *lift up your heads*. Why? Redemption is close by. The Lord of Glory will soon appear!

3. *Watch and pray (Mark 13:33)* – be diligent, walk with God, being in continuous communication with Him, allowing the Lord to take you by the hand, and walk with you along the journey, *For the Lord your God, will hold your right hand, saying to you, 'Fear not, I will help you' (Isaiah 41:13).*

4. *Love God will all your heart; love each other; by this all will know that you are followers of the Carpenter of Nazareth (Matthew 22:36-40; John 13:34,35)* – the whole Christian experience comes down to these three components. To love God is to personally know Him through Jesus Christ our Lord; to love each other (believers, as well as your neighbors) is proof that you are loving God; all will know, by your lifestyle, even when you are out of fellowship with God, that you are really a follower of God. The evidence will spill everywhere. Others will be affected by your life.

Time is short; Life is precious & Jesus is coming soon!

Chapter 3
Battle of Gog and Magog

In the book of Ezekiel we find a prophecy regarding a fierce battle that will take place in the end of time. In fact, many theologians believe that it will culminate during the 7-year Tribulation period of the world. This battle is generally called the "Battle of Gog and Magog." The prophet lists a coalition of nations and a leader of this coalition. However, the exact location of some of these nations is debated. Nevertheless, we have a good idea as to what will take place in the future regarding these nations.

In chapters 36 & 37 Ezekiel reveals to us the miraculous regathering and restoration of Israel in the last days. Chapters 38 & 39 describe a horrible battle that takes place against the restored nation. The reason for this battle, according to the prophets, is that Israel, especially Jerusalem, will become the center of attention for the world in the latter days.

Ezekiel outlines the coalition of nations that come against Israel. We learn that God intervenes and Israel is gloriously saved from utter destruction. However, there is great carnage as a result of this battle. The question before us in this article is, "Who are these nations and why will they attack Israel?"

The answer as to why they come against Israel is found in verses 10-12 of chapter 38. There will be a time when Israel believes she is dwelling in safety and relative peace. Her walls of defense are down and she is duped into believing that all is well. (This could very well be because of the treaty created by the Antichrist, Daniel 9:27).

Let us take look at this coalition of nations:

1. **Magog** (verse 2): References the territory that is located in Southern Russia around the Black Sea. Other historians say that Magog refers also to parts of southern Europe. Magog was a son of Japheth (Gen. 10:2; 1 Chron. 1:5). **Gog** (verse 2): refers to the leader of this coalition.

2. **Chief Prince** (verse 2): The Hebrew word for "Chief" is *"Rosh"*. Better translated, "Prince of Rosh." Some scholars say that "Rosh" refers to Russia.

3. **Meshech** and **Tubal** (verse 2): These were also sons of Japheth (Gen. 10:2). They settled in an area that today is called Turkey. These descendants also settled the eastern parts of Europe and southern Russia. Some suggest that Meshech refers to the area surrounding modern day Moscow and that Tubal refers to the area of modern day Tobolsk. However, it can be a stretch to give modern names to Meshech and Tubal because they sound similar to these two modern day cities. In the time of Ezekiel this area would have been in and around Turkey.

4. **Persia** (verse 5): Iran (from the east).

5. **Ethiopia** (verse 5): (from the south).

6. **Libya** (verse 5): (from the west).

7. **Gomer/Togarmah** (verse 6): Northern & Eastern Turkey (from the north).

8. **Sheba/Dedan** (verse 13): Arabian Peninsula. They will seemingly protest the battle.

9. **Tarshish** (verse 13): Refers to the western part of the Mediterranean area. Tarshish will also protest the attack.

Those nations that attack Israel will be defeated as God intervenes. Some believe, with this coalition out of the way the Antichrist will make his move and gain his maximum control over the world. – taken from Dr. Johnson's book, *"He Made the Stars Also"*

As today's events unfold in the Middle East May we realize that God is in control and that His plan will be fulfilled as it pertains to Israel and the Church. As we consider this prophesy we understand that such a war is not beyond modern day scope. Knowing that one day a coalition of nations surrounding Israel, led by a leader from the north, will attempt to overthrow her, we should pray for Israel and assist her in any way possible. May God help us to bless Israel! (Gen. 12:1-3)

Until He Lord comes we have a mandate to bless Israel and to pray for the peace of Jerusalem (Genesis12:3; Psalm 122:6).

Israel Today Ministries feeds Israelis who are hungry. Over 30% of Israeli children are in need of food. Help us bless these children and families in need!

Your tax-deductible donations are needed now! **Be a sustainer of our ministry** by giving generously every month, or at least a one-time donation. Bless Israel and you will be blessed!

Pray for Louise and me as we travel throughout the Middle East and North America presenting the gospel of God's redeeming grace through Jesus Christ our Lord to Abraham's seed.

Send your gift today and may God bless you and your family in profound and wonderful ways as you bless Israel through Israel Today Ministries!

Until He comes, we are
Together Under His Wings,

Jeffrey D. Johnson
Founder/Director

Time is short, Life is precious and Jesus is coming soon!